Fellowship of Christian Athletes presents the... ROLE MODEL SERIES

CHARLIE WARD

WINNING BY HIS GRACE

BY CHARLIE WARD WITH JOE COONEY

Sports Publishing Inc.
Champaign, Illinois 61820

Production Director: Susan M. McKinney
Cover and interior design: Julie L. Denzer

Left front cover photo courtesy of Florida State University
Right front cover photo by George Kalinsky

ISBN: 1-57167-242-7

SPORTS PUBLISHING INC.
804 N. Neil
Champaign, IL 61820
www.SportsPublishingInc.com

Printed in the United States

DEDICATION

All thanks and praise to the Lord and Savior,
Jesus Christ, for His stability in my life.

To my wife, Tonja, the love of my life and my #1
fan and friend. Thanks for all the support and
communication throughout the years.

To my mother and father...thanks for the living
example that you've given me and my brothers
and sisters.

To my brothers and sisters: Bernard; Leta; Shelia;
Carla; Chad and Charita...thank you for your love
and wisdom that we've shared over the years.

And to my friends...thank you for being there for
me, for all the prayers, and for your kindness in
good times and in bad.

Americans have always possessed a fanatical fascination and adulation for those athletes talented and blessed enough to make it in the world of professional sports. And most of these "star" ballplayers revel in the limelight and relish playing the role of "celebrity."

In Charlie Ward's case, however, one finds an enigma of the sports world. The former Florida State University football star, Heisman Trophy winner, and now a professional basketball player in his third year with the New York Knicks is the opposite of everything that is associated today with what it means to be a celebrity.

In a world known more for loud "trash talk" and egotistical boasting, 27-year-old Charlie Ward stands out with his reserved, unassuming nature and lifestyle. He is a quiet man. A man at peace, maintaining a lifestyle that is based on high ethical standards, integrity and character.

The combination of these virtues and his firm belief in God have created in him a strong and focused disposition. There is nothing "in your face" about Charlie Ward. He is not a flashy star, and he doesn't seek the spotlight. But he does eagerly accept the responsibility of a role model.

Which makes him unique. And special.

Charlie Ward is the grandson of a minister and the son of educators Willard and Charlie Ward, Sr. Charlie grew up in Thomasville, Georgia, the third of seven children in a home filled with love and all of the morals, inspiration and motivation that have become a part of who he is.

Charlie began his athletic career playing football at FSU where his talents remained hidden on the bench for the first three years. In his senior year in 1993, however, he earned the role as the starting quarterback and showed the world what a gifted athlete he truly is. His final year was a whirlwind of broken records, a national championship and the Heisman Trophy (which he won by the largest voting margin in the history of the award).

Charlie was a two-sport man in college, displaying his awesome athletic ability on the basketball court as well. In 1992 Charlie, along with teammates—and now fellow NBA stars Sam Cassell, Doug Edwards and Bob Sura, led the 1992 FSU team to its first NCAA Elite Eight appearance. He culminated his collegiate career by garnering several national awards for football, as well as being named MVP at the NCAA Basketball Tournament in the NABC college All-Star game.

In addition to his athletic successes, Charlie excelled in the classroom as well, earning his Bachelor of Arts degree with honors in his major, therapeutic recreation.

Charlie was selected in the first round of the 1994 draft by the New York Knicks, making him the first Heisman Trophy-winning quarterback in the NBA. Although he was voted MVP of the '94 NBA Doral Arrowood summer league, his first season with the Knicks was a year of learning and observing and not much playing time. But during the 1995-96 season, he began to see the light of day and exploded onto the scene with his consistent performances in the Knicks' run to the Eastern Conference semifinals. The 1996-97 season saw even more playing time for Charlie, and as the 1997-98 season began Ward was named to the starting lineup.

Charlie's work off the court is his other career. And just as his abilities benefit his team during the season, his commitment to others in his community and across the country has helped countless individuals.

Through the years Charlie has ungrudgingly dedicated hundreds of hours to community service and charitable organizations. He has spoken to many youth groups, has been instrumental in starting numerous basketball camps and has set up several summer camps of all kinds, including one for children from abusive homes. He is a member of Big Brothers/Big Sisters and makes sure to spend quality time with his Little Brother every week.

Other groups that have benefitted from Charlie's generous spirit include the Fellowship of Christian Athletes, the YMCA (in Thomasville, Georgia and Stamford, Connecticut), the United Way, "Say No To Drugs" and "Stay In School" campaigns, the Boys & Girls Clubs of New York, the Epilepsy Foundation of Florida and many, many more.

Charlie and his wife, Tonja Harding Ward, got married in the summer of 1995. They met during Charlie's senior year in college while she was attending law school at the University of Miami. Tonja is now a sports attorney working for a sports management company called Flick2, based in New York City. "I'm blessed to have such a lovely and spiritual wife," Charlie says. "I don't know where I would be without her. It's good to know you have a strong wife with Christian values—values that we share deeply. It brings us closer together."

Tonja says about Charlie, "He's my partner. He helps keep me focused. It's a blessing to have Charlie in my life."

Charlie Ward is a man of uncompromising values who also happens to possess the athletic abilities that make him a celebrity.

But Charlie will not succumb to the bright lights of the big city. He will quietly go his way, giving to his sport and giving to others. And in the end he will shine brighter than any "star."

CHARLIE WARD'S
ANNUAL CHRISTIAN BASKETBALL CAMPS

For Boys: @ Family First Sports Park, Erie, PA   (Every July)

- Indoor and Outdoor Courts with fundamental teaching stations
- Agility and quickness drills
- Contests
- Daily league play
- Guest speakers from the NBA
- Commuter & Overnight accommodations
- Quality instruction from high school coaches and college athletes
- Daily Bible Study
- Rap Sessions

For more information call (814) 866-5425

For Girls: (Every August)

- Indoor Courts with fundamental teaching stations
- Agility and quickness drills
- Contests
- Daily league play
- Guest speakers from the ABL, WNBA, NBA & business professionals
    - Topics include: Etiquette, Self-esteem, Appearance & Career Planning
- Day Camp
- Quality instruction from high school coaches and college athletes
- Daily Devotion

For more information call (212) 564-8044

TABLE OF CONTENTS

■ ■ ■ ■ ■ ■ ■ ■ ■

DEAR TEAMMATE IN CHRIST,

Welcome to the inaugural edition of the Fellowship of Christian Athletes Role Model Series. We are excited to share the Good News of Jesus Christ through the inspiring stories of some of the biggest names in the world of sports.

For over 43 years, thousands of athletes and coaches have carried the FCA torch. They have touched and influenced many lives through our Huddle program in the schools and the FCA Camps in the summer.

The first FCA Summer Camp was held in 1956 in Estes Park, Colorado. We now have over 100 Camps at 40 locations around the country.

Your purchase of this book is helping to send a young person to one of our Summer Camps where he or she will experience a life-changing week. Thank you for your contribution. We hope you enjoy this book and will share it with others.

By His Grace,

DAL SHEALY
PRESIDENT, FELLOWSHIP OF CHRISTIAN ATHLETES

RECRUITING A TEAM

But by the grace of God I am what I am, and His grace to me was not without effect. (I CORINTHIANS 15:10)

As a way of saying hello and introducing myself, I want you to focus on the above quote from the Bible. I think this quote tells us that we are all the same in God's eyes. BY HIS GRACE WE ARE WHAT WE ARE. And if we embrace His word and blessings, and if we work hard, listen well, learn from others and live a good life, we will all be the same: GOOD PEOPLE DOING GOOD THINGS.

I'm going to tell you the story of my life. Well, it's my life so far, anyway—I'm only 27, and I hope to be around to spread the Good Word for the next 60 years or more! And I hope that my sharing a few stories about my life might help you as you get on with yours. Even though I may be 10, or 15, or maybe 20 years older than you, remember that we all are the same in certain ways. We are all human beings, and we all pretty much want the same things in life. We want to be happy. We want to be loved. We want to love and help others.

Perhaps you'll learn a couple things after reading this book. Perhaps you'll take a few lessons with you.

Charlie Ward
Point guard for the New York Knicks

Here I am with my mom, Willard Ward, my dad, Charlie Ward Sr., and my sister Leta.

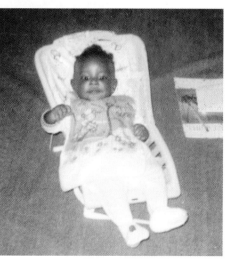

I was six months old in 1971.

You may think that because I'm older, I don't really remember what it's like to be a kid. But that's not true. I do remember my childhood. And I **do** recall all of the different feelings and emotions you have when you're growing up.

Some of my fondest memories of growing up are of the true spirit of togetherness that my family shared. I often look back on those times—as far back as I can remember—and I am always filled with a sense of warmth and comfort. And I feel very blessed and proud that I experienced the kind of childhood that I did.

I certainly had a great family. We were a real team that stuck together through thick and thin, the good times and the bad. And believe me, there were more "thin" times, than "thick," if you know what I mean. We weren't rich by any means. But my father and mother worked hard to make sure we had just enough. We did have food on the table, and we did have clothes on our backs. We certainly didn't have any luxuries, and we definitely didn't have any great electronic games back then...and remember—even though I'm not *that* much older than you—we didn't have Nintendo, MTV, computers or any of the cool stuff that a lot of young kids have today. All those things weren't even invented yet!

The Ward family

Here I am sitting on my Grandma Agnes' lap while my Aunt Helen Ward looks on.

As I said, growing up we didn't have all that much—you could say we were in the lower middle class. But my mother and father were both teachers, and even though they worked very hard all day, they then had to come home to me and my five brothers and sisters.

I'm holding the ball in this photo while my sister Leta (holding the doll) and I play with the neighbors.

My sisters Leta (posed), and Shelia (lower front), and I (holding football) playing with relatives.

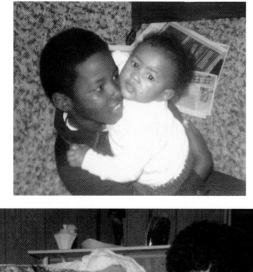

Getting a hug from my little sister Carla.

As the only brother at the time, I was coerced into playing "dress-up" with my sisters, Leta and Shelia.

What carried us through was the tremendous amount of patience my parents had. They never complained about really not having money to provide for us, and they let us know what we could and couldn't have. That's just the way it was. We couldn't have $100 shoes, and we certainly did not conform to the world in fashion. You didn't find any brand names on the clothes of the Ward children. But we did have each other. And we had a loving, trusting and caring environment.

The lesson to be learned here is: YOU REALLY DON'T HAVE TO HAVE A LOT OF MONEY, FLASHY CLOTHES OR GAMES TO WIN IN THE GAME OF LIFE. You can get by, and you can win by being a good person and doing the right things.

And I understand that some kids don't have both parents around. Or maybe you don't have brothers and sisters. And I know that when times get tough you may think you're never going to be able to be happy. **BUT THERE ARE PEOPLE OUT THERE WHO CAN HELP YOU.** Your teachers, your friends' parents, your priest or minister at your church.

I was in the fifth grade in 1979.

And then there is the greatest helper of all. The best coach in the world—the Lord.

When I was a kid our family went to church all the time. And although you don't want to go sometimes—maybe you're playing or watching a basketball game on TV—I promise you that you will appreciate it later. BEING AROUND THE WORD OF THE LORD HELPS YOU GET THROUGH THE TOUGH TIMES. You learn from it.

Here I am at 11 years old in 1979-80.

On Christmas morning, 1981 with my sisters and brother (from left), Carla, Charita, and Chad.

I remember going to Sunday school at church where we learned Bible stories and how to pray. At home my parents helped us to learn the scriptures. And every Sunday we had Bible study at home, too. The whole family would get together, and each week a different family member would read from a different part of the Bible. We would talk about what we learned at church or Sunday school class.

And that's how I first got on the Lord's team. And I'll tell you something: WITH THE LORD AS MY COACH, I HAVE A CHAMPIONSHIP SEASON EVERY YEAR OF MY LIFE.

Those times certainly were helpful to me, and they shaped me as the person I am today. It was a fellowship with the family, and it brought us closer together especially with the word of God. We learned to love each other and respect each other. And we learned this by the examples our parents set.

My friend, Jeff Bryant, and I in June of 1982.

Train a child in the way he should go, and when he is old he will not turn from it.
(PROVERBS 22:6)

My eighth grade class picture.

The Ward children—seated: Carla and Charita, second row: Shelia and Chad, third row: me and Leta

There were certainly times when I got into mischief. I wasn't a total angel! No kid is. I remember that there were times I wanted to experience different things, or I wanted to go out and play when I was supposed to be doing chores. And I'd get into trouble and make mistakes. **BUT I LEARNED FROM THOSE MISTAKES.** And my parents were always quick with a lesson when I stepped out of line.

Hard work never hurt anybody. I always wanted to play, but we still had to help out around the house. My daddy used to say that's why he and my mom had all us kids—he had dishwashers, someone to clean the kitchen, and cut the grass.

And we also had to do well in school. I remember at age eight I was struggling with my studies. I was in third grade and I didn't really like reading. I was really only interested in sports. In fact, my mother worried that I might even have a learning disability. But she says one day she heard me reading the highlights of a football game and explaining everything to my father. She quickly realized that I was just being lazy. And boy, did she get on me.

A family portrait—first row: Charlie Sr., Chad, Willard, Charita, Carla; seond row: Leta, me, and Shelia.

She thought I just didn't want to learn, which wasn't really true. But she told me that I had to try harder—or else! And when my mother said that, we moved pretty quick. My grades improved in no time. My mother taught me a lesson, and I learned how important it is to do well in school. **YOUR EDUCATION IS NOT SOMETHING TO BE TAKEN FOR GRANTED. LEARN ALL YOU CAN AND BE THE BEST THAT YOU CAN.** If you're having trouble, talk to your mom and dad, or your teacher. Even your friends. They can help you out too.

My ninth grade class picture.

I was on crutches after knee surgery in 1986.

I did a science project about knee injuries (mine in particular) in school that year.

And if things get really bad, look to the Lord. He's not only a great coach, but a great teacher.

It says in the book of Romans in the Bible: **"If God is for you, then who can be against you."** Remember this the next time you're struggling and having a hard time, and you think that life's unfair, or the whole world is against you. GOD IS WITH YOU, AND HE CAN HELP YOU GET THROUGH ANYTHING.

My grandfathers passed away within a few years of each other when I was between seven and nine years old. I really loved my grandfathers, and it was very hard to lose them. One of my grandfathers had a paint and body shop—where he repaired cars—and I remember that he used to take us there and we'd pretend we were helping him. And my other grandfather was a minister, and he used to own orange groves—what a great place to play! The memories—even though I was so young—are great about my grandfathers.

And it was difficult to lose someone you love. But it's something that has come to pass, and the more you learn about the word of God, you know they're in a better place. It's tough, though, when you're young. And it's hard to understand. But you **can** and **will** get through it.

Celebrating my sister Shelia's birthday in 1989. Chad and Charita are in muscle poses; Carla and I are in the background.

PRACTICE — PRACTICE — PRACTICE

When I first started to play sports—football, baseball and basketball—I quickly learned the importance of practice. To win a big game, or to have a good season, you must practice hard. To get to know the game. To get to know the other players on your team. To get better you have to practice.

To win at the game of life you also have to practice. You need to work at being a good person. You need to make an effort to help others, and get along with others. And you need to have a heart that pleases God.

Here I'm with Mom and Dad at my FSU Student Government Vice President Installation in the 1992-93 academic year.

My future wife, Tonja, and I in 1993.

As it says in the Bible...**Just as each of us has one body with many members and these members do not all have the same function, so in Christ we who are many form one body, and each member belongs to all of the others. We have different gifts according to the grace given us. (ROMANS 12:4-6)**

God has given all of us many different talents, but we still have to work together. Getting along with others is a very important part of life. The examples you set—and what you learn from others—will be key to your success.

I grew up in a small town in Georgia called Thomasville. I started organized sports in the fifth grade, playing football and basketball at the local YMCA in my town. My parents really didn't want me to start playing sports so soon. I guess they thought it would affect my school work. BUT I STUDIED HARD AND PRACTICED HARD, AND I WAS ABLE TO BALANCE THE TWO.

Taking time out with a young fan in 1993.

It was very rewarding playing quarterback for Florida State University. (Photo courtesy of FSU)

One of the first things I learned when playing sports was the importance of getting along with other people. YOU SIMPLY NEED TO BE ABLE TO WORK WELL WITH OTHERS AND COME TOGETHER AS A TEAM.

You need to get along with others off the basketball court and football field, too. And there's a lot involved with that. As you get older, you'll find a lot of pressures from others your age to do things that you think are wrong. Or maybe they'll say that if you don't do something that makes you "uncool." We all want to "fit in" with the crowd. But if you have a feeling something is wrong, then you should go with that feeling.

(Photo by Ryals Lee)

Peer pressure is a lot to handle. I know that. I once had a friend who was in the same club as I was at school. And he had gone with some other guys to smoke marijuana. I simply walked away—BECAUSE I KNEW IT WAS WRONG—and I didn't hang out with them. I just made it a point to stay away from any of the kids who might be drinking alcohol or doing drugs.

This was taken in my senior year at Florida State University. (Photo courtesy of FSU)

I did once try some alcohol, and it turned out to be a very good lesson.

One night my parents were out and my Grandmom was home at our house to watch over us. But my older sister, my younger sister, my cousin and I snuck off to another part of the house and I found some white wine. I started drinking the wine because, even though the others told me not to, I wanted to try it.

Well...I got so sick and dizzy you wouldn't believe it! I was only about 11 or 12 years old and I remember that right then and there I told myself that I didn't like alcohol and would never again drink any.

Playing in the Orange Bowl against Nebraska on January 1, 1993. (Photo by Ross Obley)

Kids and teenagers just shouldn't even try alcohol or drugs. They will only make you sick. Wait until you're over 21 and then, when you are an adult, you can make up your own mind about what you do.

There will always be temptations to do certain things. BUT JUST REMEMBER THAT GOD WILL NOT LET YOU BE TEMPTED BEYOND WHAT YOU CAN BEAR. And when you are tempted He will also provide a way out so that you can stand up under it. But if you live by God's word, your decision will not be hard.

As you get older, the temptations increase. Peer pressure again. And as you get older new worlds open themselves up to you. When I went off to college at Florida State University, I got caught up in the partying ways of college life. But the Lord helped me through that. It was a very trying time, but God—as my coach— brought me through it. I wasn't living the life, a true life, of being a Christian person. Some of my morals fell a bit.

I wasn't drinking or doing drugs, but I just wasn't leading a good life.

But the Lord allowed me to come back. Everyone makes mistakes and GOD WILL FORGIVE YOU FOR MISTAKES. But you have to learn from them. If you mess up, and then go out carousing again, you are going back to the old life...you can't do that.

(Photo courtesy of FSU)

There was a scandal that shook Florida State's football program when I was there. When players excel at sports in college, professional agents try to get in contact with the players in order to tempt them to sign with the agents when they leave college. The players are targeted by representatives of the agents who try to tempt future clients by sending them on shopping sprees, giving them money, clothes, shoes. It happens, but it's wrong, and it's against the law. Sure, their offers looked tempting, but I just turned and walked away whenever I was approached. Other players gave in to the temptation...I didn't. You shouldn't either.

Here I am calling plays against Kansas on August 28, 1993. (Photo courtesy of FSU)

On the move. (Photo courtesy of FSU)

I have always loved playing sports, and I thank the Lord for blessing me with the talent to play well. As I mentioned before, I played basketball, football and baseball when I was a kid. When I got into high school, I did very well as the quarterback for my team, and I was even named Georgia's top prep quarterback in 1987.

When I went to college at Florida State, I figured I'd play quarterback for them too. But I had to wait on the bench my first couple of years while the older quarterbacks played. Since I wasn't really playing on the football team, I played basketball. And because of my God-given talents I was able to help our team do pretty well. In fact, in the 1991-92 season our basketball team had a record of 22 wins and 10 losses. And the next year we went 25-10.

Finally, in my junior year at FSU, I got a chance to be the starting quarterback, and I was very excited to play. However, I didn't start off that well. In fact, in the first two games I threw eight interceptions... pretty terrible. It took a while, but then I had a successful season, setting a single-season record for individual offense.

I wasn't upset when I started out badly.

In the Florida State vs. Tulane game on November 14, 1992. (Photo by Ross Obley)

Because I had patience.

**Having an interview with Lynn Swann.
(Photo courtesy of FSU)**

As it says in the Bible, **"it is good to wait quietly for the salvation of the Lord."** That means you have to have patience. In everything you do. And if you work hard and study hard, good things will come to you.

I always start out slow. That's been my track record, so to speak, starting off slow. Especially when I haven't played in a while. But all throughout my career God has given me the ability to over-come obstacles.

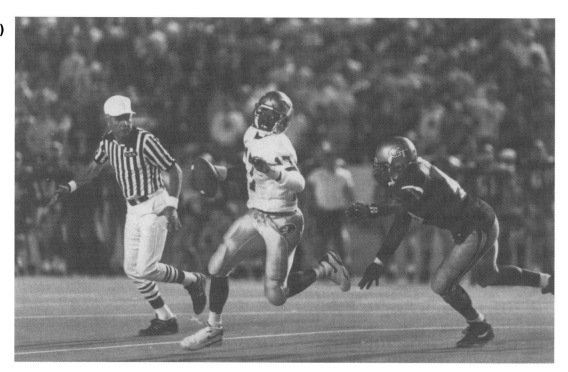

While I was at FSU I also joined the Fellowship of Christian Athletes. I was grateful to find such a group. The FCA gave me a way to hear the word of the Lord and team up with other believers. We met during the week in what we called "huddles," you know, like when you're on the football field. It was kind of like going to church in the middle of the week. I enjoyed it and it brought me to a point where I enjoyed the Word along with some of my teammates.

As you may know, my senior year in college was quite an experience for me. Our team won the national championship, and I was named the best college football player in the country. That was really quite an honor. And I was proud of my accomplishments.

But winning the Heisman Trophy also made me more humble. I realize and understand it was a blessing to me. I wasn't about to go around bragging about it, or thinking I was better than others. There's never been a point in my life where I lost focus of who I was and what God has allowed me to accomplish. I've never lost focus of that aspect of my life.

As it says in the Bible in **PHiLiPPiANS 2**: **...If you have any encouragement from being united with Christ, if any comfort from His love, if any fellowship with the Spirit, if any tenderness and compassion, then make my joy complete by being like-minded, having the same love, being one in spirit and purpose. Do nothing out of any selfish ambition or vain conceit, but in humility consider others better than yourselves. Each of you should look not only to your own interests, but also to the interests of others. Your attitude should be the same as that of Christ Jesus.**

I also enjoyed basketball while at Florida State. (Photo courtesy of FSU)

THE GAME PLAN

The Ward family (left to right): Shelia, Leta, Chad, Mom, Charlie, Dad, Charita, Bernard and Carla.

SEE: **Charlie's** HEISMAN HERE!

THOMAS COUNTY PUBLIC LIBRARY

Thomas County Public Library is the home of my Heisman Trophy.

Another quote from the Bible in **COLOSSIANS 3:23**: **Whatever you do, work at it with all your heart, as working for the Lord, not for men.**

When I graduated college—and after winning the Heisman Trophy—a lot of people thought that I would just go straight to the National Football League.

Things didn't quite work out that way, however.

I thank God for giving me the skills and the options to play basketball over football. I didn't become overly concerned over whether I was going to play football or basketball. I'm not the type of person to worry about my future because **I KNOW IT'S IN GOD'S HANDS.**

It's truly a blessing to be playing basketball. God gave me the talent to play and this is my way to spread His glory.

I was drafted by the New York Knicks in 1994. I only played in 10 games for a total of 48 minutes in my rookie year with the Knicks. But again, I was patient. And it was a good experience, adapting to the changes of playing in the NBA. As always, the patience paid off. I got to play in 62 games in my second year and in my third year I saw action in 79 games, missing only three regular season contests.

And for the 1997-98 season I was blessed to have been named the starting point guard. And I worked very hard to contribute to the success of the team.

(Photo courtesy of FSU)

It took a lot of work to get accustomed to playing in the NBA. My first year in New York I had to study hard to learn the offensive system the team had. Teams are always changing their strategies and systems, so during the next two years I had to learn a new system all over again. Gradually, I began to play a lot more. And through hard work, patience and a lot of practice, I improved as a player and as a person who knows the game.

(Photo by George Kalinsky)

Every Thanksgiving, Tonja and I like to join my Knicks teammates in sharing the holiday with others. At right, here I am with my teammates Herb Williams (middle) and John Starks (right) as we serve my favorite Thanksgiving dessert, delicious pumpkin pie. (Photos by George Kalinsky)

A big reason why I got better was the support and advice I got from my friend and teammate Derek Harper. I was very fortunate and blessed that he was a part of my progress and life because I learned so much from him as a player and as a person. And you can't take that away. He taught me about work ethic, which helped me become more disciplined. In basketball, there were a lot of things he taught me as far as moves, tricks, and short cuts. But basically he taught me about being professional, a good professional. He didn't miss practices, he didn't miss games, and if he missed practice, something had to be really, really wrong.

You can always learn from others. No matter how old you are or how successful. So LOOK TO YOUR FRIENDS, FAMILIES AND TEACHERS. THEY CAN ALWAYS TEACH YOU SOMETHING ABOUT BEING A BETTER PERSON.

The first couple of years were tough in the NBA, but I kept looking back to another quote from the Bible that helped me get prepared.

From **EPHESIANS 6:10-12, 14-15**:

...be strong in the Lord and in His mighty power...put on the full armor of God so that you can take your stand against the devil's schemes...stand firm then, with the belt of truth buckled around your waist, with the breastplate of righteousness in place, and with your feet fitted with the readiness that comes with the gospel of peace.

It is always important to be prepared for the challenges and obstacles you'll have to overcome in life. If you are a member of the Boy Scouts, or if you know about the Boy Scouts, you'll know that their motto is: **ALWAYS BE PREPARED.**

Speaking at the Thomasville Library where my Heisman is on display.

Because you never know what life is going to throw you. And it is also very important to remember that you're not always going to be on top. I've seen players who were very good and very successful, but then they get injured. Or they just can't play as well as they used to.

And you know what happens? They get depressed and upset if they can't play anymore. And then they look for someone to blame. Or someone to yell at.

All because they weren't prepared. IF YOU ARE THE BEST THAT YOU CAN BE, YOU'LL BE PREPARED. And if you are successful, that's absolutely great. But know that "stars" don't shine forever. You are not going to be always on top. And when you're on the bottom, you need the strength to get back up again.

I love reading so much that every chance I get I urge others to read too. (Photo by George Kalinsky)

Ceremony retiring my football jersey. (First time Florida State retired jersey of an active player.) I was honored at the jersey presentation by Florida State University's Assistant Athletic Director, Wayne Hogan (right) and Coach Bobby Bowden (left).

have that strength because I don't doubt myself. I never have and I never will. If anyone else does I'll just have to go out and prove them wrong. I'll be prepared for anything. And whether I'm playing basketball or teaching kids, or whatever I do, I know that I'LL BE THE BEST I CAN BE.

Here my parents are attending Central High School's ceremony retiring my jersey. Thomas County named a street after me and presented road signs now posted at all highway entries into the county announcing that Thomas County is the "Home of Charlie Ward Jr." I was very humbled and appreciative of these honors.

I was once quoted in a newspaper article saying, "I feel like I want everyone to be like me. Not just on the basketball court but in life, period."

That may sound a bit arrogant. Not too humble. But what I was trying to say was that I truly feel that I am on a winning team. Life's winning team. Why?

Because I HAVE THE LORD AS MY COACH. Not just on the basketball court. Or on the football field. But in life. Period.

While teaching at my camps, I was better able to appreciate the fact that young women play just as well and as much as the guys. They should be given more opportunities to showcase their talents. (Photo by George Kalinsky)

There are many lessons to be learned. There is much to do. The basic principles for life survival are these:

STICKS AND STONES MAY BREAK YOUR BONES, BUT NAMES WILL NEVER HURT YOU. If someone calls you the worst name in the book, show them who's the bigger person and walk away. It is not always easy, but you should *always* take the high road.

The law of the universe says that what goes around comes around. If you do good, it will come back to you. If you don't, well...think about it.

ALWAYS DO THE BEST YOU CAN and live with your mistakes as well as forgive your regrets.

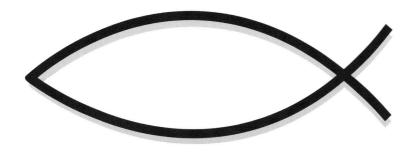

Keep the faith. Have absolute faith in God and in yourself. FAITH IS ALWAYS BEING TESTED, which is why it's important to keep your faith renewed through prayer, spiritual readings and examples.

I try to read the Bible as often as I can. Of course, we travel a lot during the season so I try to spend as many of those long hours on plane and bus trips by catching up on reading my favorite passages and looking for new ones.

One of the ways I like to help spread the good messages of the Lord is by passing out copies of the "Daily Word." These are inspirational messages—about living a good life, about helping others, about being humble, about passing it on—that are real life examples of what the Bible says.

With my family at graduation from Florida State University in December 1993. From left to right: Grandmother (Agnes Ward), Leta, Dad, Shelia, Carla, me, Mom, Charita, and Chad.

carry these daily messages with me always. And I hand them out to my teammates on the Knicks every day that we're together. I give it to all of the members of the Knicks. Whether they read it or not, that's up to them. But I hope they do.

Accepting the 1994 Charlie Sullivan Award (Other nominees included Gail Devers, Dan Jansen, Sheryl Swoopes, and Shannon Miller).

It was a revelation from God to start prayers after the games.
Plus, I believe a family that prays together stays together.
(Dad used to always say that.) (Photo by George Kalinsky)

After every game I also invite and encourage all my teammates—and even the guys from the other team we played—to join in on a prayer huddle after the final buzzer. You may have seen the football players in the NFL doing this after games. I just think it's a great way for the guys to come together and thank the Lord for the talents He has bestowed on us. My teammate, Buck Williams, and I feel it's really important the people see our "huddles" after each game. Hopefully, it even gets on television. Because I think: Why do people watch us anyway? So we can sell jerseys? We have a lot of pull in this society and we should step up and show people that LIFE IS MORE THAN JUST BASKETBALL.

Win or lose, we get together. Sure, I can be upset or angry if we've lost the game, or if I've played poorly. But I know that life goes on after I step off the court. **IF YOU PLAY SPORTS, REMEMBER THAT WINNING AND LOSING IS ALL PART OF THE GAME.** When you've worked hard, and your team has worked together to win a game, that's great! But don't get arrogant or big-headed and rub it in anybody's face. **WIN WITH DIGNITY.**

Our wedding day, August 26, 1995.

And if you find that the other team was better than yours, ACCEPT THE LOSS WITH DIGNITY. If you do your best and try your hardest—at anything you do— even if you fail you can learn from your mistakes, try a little harder next time, and keep your head up.

I'd like to close with just a few more messages I'd like to pass on...

DON'T IDOLIZE HEROES. I really don't have any heroes or idols except my parents and Jesus Christ. There are role models in life that you should look up to and try to copy by example. But don't put anyone on a pedestal, either. Everyone is human. And HUMANS MAKE MISTAKES.

I don't consider myself a role model because I play professional basketball. I am a role model because I have sisters and brothers, nieces and nephews, god-children and young people—someone who is always looking up to me. Therefore, I HAVE TO CONDUCT MYSELF IN A FASHION THAT PLEASES ME, GOD AND OTHERS. You should do the same.

Maybe there are those of us who get caught up in this image of what we're supposed to be, but are not accountable for our actions.

Remember that YOU SHOULD LIVE YOUR LIFE TO PLEASE GOD, and when you do that, those negative incidents that happen won't affect your life too much. Hang in there. And don't ever forget that...

WITH THE LORD AS YOUR COACH, YOU CAN'T LOSE.

FCA SUMMER CAMPS

WHAT IS IT?

- Intense athletic instruction and competition
- Inspirational speakers
- Small group time
- Life-long friendships

WHAT ARE THE TYPES OF CAMPS OFFERED?

~~~~~~~~~Athletic~~~~~~~~~

~~~~~~~~Sports~~~~~~~~

~~~Leadership~~~

~~~Coaches~~~

WHY FCA CAMP?

- The best instruction from college and professional coaches and athletes
- Small group time with college athletes
- You'll be challenged in ways you never have been before
- Develop practical skills to be a true leader in your daily life
- Tackle real life issues you deal with every day

WHAT IS FCA?

The Fellowship of Christian Athletes is an interdenominational Christian organization that for more than 40 years has been focused on the purpose: "To present to athletes and coaches, and all whom they influence, the challenge and adventure of receiving Jesus Christ as Savior and Lord, serving Him in their relationships and in the fellowship of the church."

For more information on the ministry of FCA, go to our home page at www.fca.org
or call 1-800-289-0909